Discovering the World Around Us

Grizzly

TJ Rob

GRIZZLY

By TJ Rob

From the Discovering The World Around Us Series, Volume 6

Copyright Text TJ Rob, 2016

All rights reserved. No part of the book may be reproduced in any form without permission in writing from the author. Reviewers may quote brief passages in review.

ISBN 978-1-988695-18-1

Disclaimer

No part of this book may be reproduced in any form or by any means, mechanical or electronic, including photocopying or recording, or by an information storage and retrieval system, or transmitted by email without permission in writing from the publisher. This book is for entertainment purposes only. The views expressed are those of author alone.

Published by

TJ Rob

Suite 609

440-10816 Macleod Trail SE

Calgary, AB T2J 5N8 www.TJRob.com

Image Credit:

pg.10 ,IUCN Red List of Threatened Species, species assessors and the authors of the spatial data. [CC BY-SA 3.0 (http://creativecommons.org/licenses/by-sa/3.0)], via Wikimedia Commons

Photo Credits: Images used under license from Shutterstock.com:

Front Cover page, Album Imagery/Shutterstock.com;Back Cover page, Bildagentur Zoonar GmbH/Shutterstock.com; pg. 1, Dennis W. Donohue/Shutterstock.com; pg. 4, Scott E Read/Shutterstock.com; pg. 5, Prazis/Shutterstock.com; pg. 6, Adam Van Spronsen/Shutterstock.com; pg. 7, Ewais/Shutterstock.com; pg. 8, Iakov Filimonov/Shutterstock.com; pg. 9, Iakov Filimonov/Shutterstock.com; pg. 11, Andreas Argirakis/Shutterstock.com; pg. 13, Dennis W. Donohue/Shutterstock.com; pg. 14, CLFProductions/Shutterstock.com; pg. 15, Andrea Izzotti/Shutterstock.com; pg. 16, Larry Jacobsen/Shutterstock.com; pg. 17, Galyna Andrushko/Shutterstock.com; pg. 18, Sergei Drozd/Shutterstock.com; pg. 18, Chad Zuber/Shutterstock.com; pg. 18, bkp/Shutterstock.com; pg. 19, Robson Abbott/Shutterstock.com; pg. 19, Michael Vigliotti/Shutterstock.com; pg. 19, Jiri Hera/Shutterstock.com; pg. 19, IrinaK/Shutterstock.com; pg. 19, nialat/Shutterstock.com; pg. 20, Lorraine Logan/Shutterstock.com; pg. 21, Gleb Tarro/Shutterstock.com; pg. 22, Scott E Read/Shutterstock.com; pg. 24, kzww/Shutterstock.com; pg. 26, Lorraine Logan/Shutterstock.com; pg. 27, kelly999/Shutterstock.com; pg. 28, Larry Jacobsen/Shutterstock.com; pg. 29, Larry Jacobsen/Shutterstock.com; pg. 31, Janvdb95/Shutterstock.com; pg. 32, Don Mammoser/Shutterstock.com; pg. 33, outdoorsman/Shutterstock.com; pg. 35, zlikovec/Shutterstock.com; pg. 37, Steve Bower/Shutterstock.com; pg. 38, Lamen Percy/Shutterstock.com; pg. 39, robert cicchetti/Shutterstock.com; pg. 41, ArCaLu/Shutterstock.com

TABLE OF CONTENTS	Page
What are Grizzlies?	4
How did Grizzlies get their name?	5
What color are Grizzlies?	6
How big is a Grizzly?	7
How to spot a Grizzly...	8
Where do Grizzlies live in the wild today?	10
Where do Grizzlies like to live?	11
How many are left in the wild?	12
Are there differences between Grizzlies and Black Bears?	14
How long do Grizzlies live?	16
What does a Grizzly eat?	17
Some of a Grizzly's favorite foods	18
How often does a Grizzly eat?	20
How do Grizzlies hunt?	23
How fast can a Grizzly run?	26
Do Grizzlies climb trees?	27
How far do Grizzlies roam?	28
What about Grizzly cubs?	30
What happens when Grizzlies hibernate in the Winter?	34
True Hibernation or something else?	36
How do Grizzlies communicate with one another?	38
Are Grizzlies dangerous?	39
Grizzly fun facts	40
Please leave a review and Other EXCITING Books by TJ Rob	42

What are Grizzlies?

Grizzlies or Grizzly Bears are part of the Brown bear family. Grizzlies are a sub-species of the Brown bear species.

Grizzlies first came to North America about 50,000 years ago. They originated in Europe or Asia.

Grizzly bears are the 3rd largest of all the bears on Earth. Only the Kodiak bear, another member of the Brown bear family, and the Polar bear are bigger.

Grizzlies are known for being very aggressive when they feel that they or their cubs are being threatened.

How did Grizzlies get their name?

The famous explorers Lewis and Clark first gave the bear its name — "grisly" or "grizzly".

There are 2 possible reasons for the name.

They could have named it after the golden and grey tips of hair that gave it a "grizzled" look.

Grizzly also could have meant "fear-inspiring".

In 1815, naturalist George Ord officially named the bear for its terrifying character.

The scientific name for Grizzlies is "Ursus Arctos Horribilis" (Brown Bear Horrible or Terrifying).

What color are Grizzlies?

A Grizzly's color ranges from nearly white to yellow to black.

Most Grizzlies have light fur on the head and shoulders, a dark body, and even darker feet and legs.

Their body shape and long fur tend to make Grizzlies look heavier than they actually are.

How big is a Grizzly?

Grizzlies are 3 to 4 feet (0.9 to 1.2 meters) tall when on all fours. When they stand on their hind legs they can be up to 8 feet (2.4 meters) tall.

Depending on the availability of food, Grizzly Bears can weigh as much as 1400 pounds (635kg). This weight is very rare.

The average weight for male Grizzlies is from 400 to 790 pounds (180 to 360kg).

Female Grizzlies weigh between 290 to 400 pounds (130 to 180kg).

How to spot a Grizzly ...

White or light colored fur on the back and sides

Darker colored legs

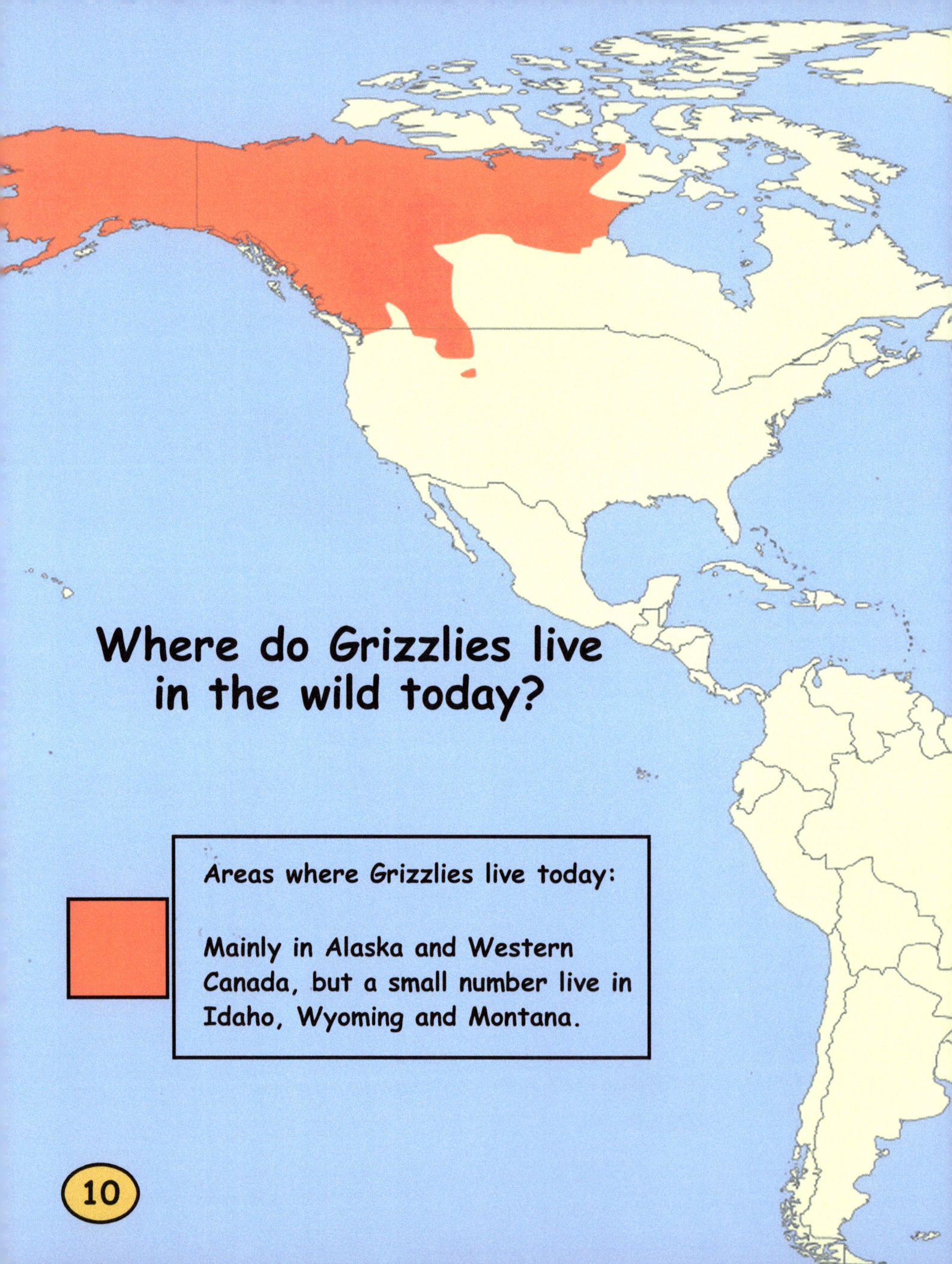

Where do Grizzlies live in the wild today?

Areas where Grizzlies live today:

Mainly in Alaska and Western Canada, but a small number live in Idaho, Wyoming and Montana.

Where do Grizzlies like to live?

Grizzlies can be found in forests, grasslands, river valleys and in mountains.

Grizzly bears build dens in protected spaces such as caves, burrows and dead trees. They use these dens for hibernation during the Winter.

In Spring, Summer and Fall, Grizzlies make day beds in forested areas that allow them to be comfortable on a hot or a cool day.

Mother Grizzlies keep their cubs hidden in shrubs and wooded areas.

How many are left in the wild?

It is estimated that there are about 50,000 to 60,000 Grizzlies in the wild.

Western and Northern Canada	20,000 — 25,000
Alaska	30,000 — 35,000
Lower 48 States of the USA	1,200 — 1,500

Grizzlies are extinct in most of the lower 48 States of the USA, and their numbers are dropping in Canada.

Grizzlies are listed as being "endangered".
"Endangered" means a species is considered in danger of extinction within all or a large portion of the area that it lives in.

Are there differences between Grizzlies and Black Bears?

Tall pointed ears

No shoulder hump

Straight face

Black Bear

Short front claws

How long do Grizzlies live?

Male Grizzlies in the wild live for about 22 years. Females live a bit longer for about 26 years.

The record for Grizzlies in the wild is 39 years. In captivity, living in zoos and animal sanctuaries, the record was 44 years.

What does a Grizzly eat?

Grizzlies can eat anything humans do, but most of their diet comes from berries, bulbs, roots, grass, fruits, nuts and insects.

They also eat rodents, fish, honey and other animals depending on where they live.

When they can catch them Grizzlies eat adult Deer, Caribou, Elk and Moose. Usually they only catch calves and newborns.

If Grizzlies find the body of a dead animal, they will eat it too.

Grizzlies use their powerful long claws to dig out and catch rodents and small mammals from their dens or holes.

Some of a Grizzly's favorite foods:

Dogwood Berries

Blueberries

Dandelions

Moose

Caribou

Kokanee Salmon

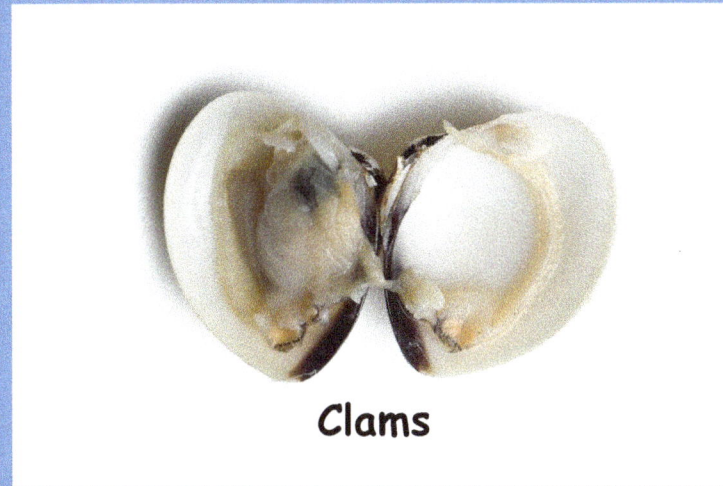
Clams

Sockeye Salmon

How often does a Grizzly eat?

The Grizzly bear spends a lot of time searching for food and eating in the late Summer and early Fall.

Bears have only about 7 months to eat enough food to last for the whole year. During hibernation the Grizzly bear doesn't eat or drink.

As Winter approaches, bears may eat for 20-23 hours a day to store enough fat to survive through hibernation.

Grizzlies will eat up to 80 to 100 pounds (36 to 45 kg) of food per day. They are able to gain 3 to 6 pounds (1.35 to 2.75 kg) in body weight in a day.

This extra food adds an extra layer of fat to its body so it can hibernate in its den for 4 to 5 months during the coldest weather.

Normally Grizzly bears are solitary animals but can be seen together with other bears when there is lots of food for everyone.

Popular fishing spots can be seen filled with many Grizzlies all fishing for Salmon at the same time.

How do Grizzlies hunt?

When searching for prey, Grizzlies use their great sense of smell by bowing their heads low to the ground and sniffing while they walk.

They stand on their hind legs to gain a better view of the area as well as to hear better.

While standing, a Grizzly turns its head and ears in all directions to scan the area.

Grizzlies are usually searching for calves that are bedded down and sleeping because these are the easiest to catch.

When a herd is found, the Grizzly hides to avoid being seen by the herd.

When a bedding calf cannot be found, a Grizzly may try to ambush an adult prey.

The bear will stalk a herd closely while remaining unseen, and attack with a sudden burst of speed.

They will focus on calves that lag behind the herd and have little protection from adults.

When the bear closes in on its prey it can knock it over with its muzzle or paw.

Often Grizzlies are seen on the edges of forests near fields and meadows waiting for herds so that they can ambush them.

How fast can a Grizzly run?

Even though Grizzly bears are extremely large they can run up to 35 miles per hour (55 km per hour), but for short distances only.

A bear can run 50 yards (45 meters) in 3 seconds flat. That's faster than a race horse for short distances, and more than twice as fast as any human.

Grizzlies can run up and down hills at full speed too.

Do Grizzlies climb trees?

Younger Grizzlies love climbing.

It was thought that because adult Grizzlies have much longer claws than Black bears, they are not able to climb trees.

This is not true.

Adult Grizzlies are able to climb, but not as well as Black bears that are better climbers.

Grizzlies have been recorded climbing 50 foot (15 meter) trees.

As Grizzlies reach adulthood they climb less and less, but will climb a tree if they have to.

How far do Grizzlies roam?

Grizzlies live in the same territory for their whole lives.

Even though Grizzlies live alone, their territories can overlap one another. Unlike other animals, Grizzlies do not stake and defend their territory.

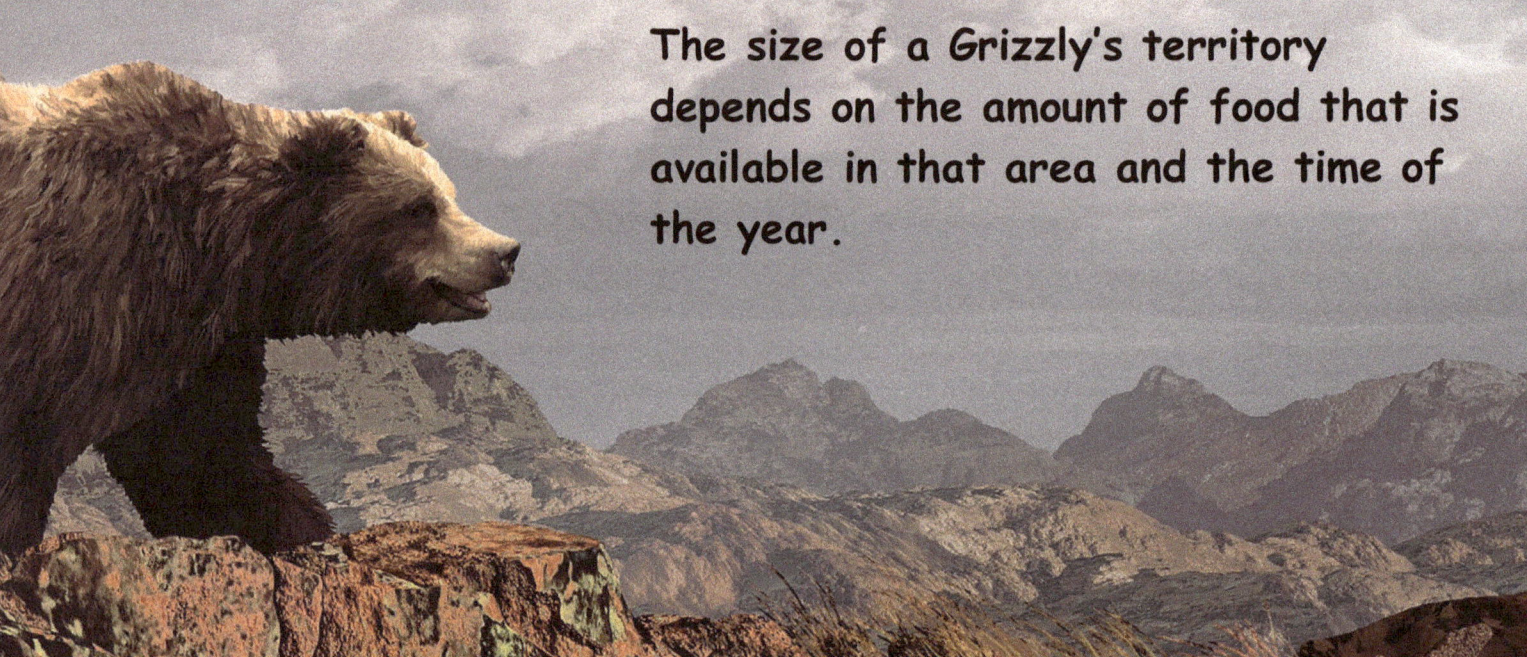

The size of a Grizzly's territory depends on the amount of food that is available in that area and the time of the year.

A food source that is plentiful in early spring often dies out by late spring, causing a bear to move to other parts of its territory.

Because the food that is available in that area changes from one year to another, the territory of a Grizzly will also change from year to year.

Male Grizzlies have a much larger roaming area than females.

Males are larger, so they need more food and a bigger area to roam to find it. Males also roam further because they need to find female Grizzlies to mate with.

Females are smaller, and eat less. They also have to watch their cubs, who are too small to roam huge areas.

A male Grizzly's roaming area can be as large as 300 to 500 square miles (775 to 1300 square km).

A female's roaming area is about 70 to 100 square miles (180 to 260 square km).

What about Grizzly cubs?

A baby Grizzly is called a cub.

Pregnant Grizzly bears give birth in their sleep in late January to early March!

Grizzly mothers have between 1 and 4 cubs at a time. The average is 2 per litter. Often they are twins.

Grizzly bear cubs are born with no teeth and no hair. They are also born blind.

At birth cubs only weigh about 1 pound (.45 kg).

For the first month, the cubs feed on their mother's milk and gain strength.

By the time Spring comes, the cubs have opened their eyes and grown teeth and fur.

In the Spring the cubs are ready to start moving out of the den.

Cubs remain with their mother for 2 to 3 years before the mother mates again and produces another litter.

Grizzly bear mothers are highly protective of their young and will fight to the death to protect them.

Female Grizzlies are able to have cubs at 5 to 6 years of age. Grizzlies have cubs every 3 years on average.

Male bears do not help to raise the young bears.

What happens when Grizzlies hibernate in the Winter?

For 4 to 5 months during Winter, Grizzly bears enter their dens and hibernate. They hibernate when there is deep snow, very cold air temperatures and not much food is available.

During this sleep period, they do not need food or water. They also do not go to the bathroom at all during these months.

They just sleep.

This deep sleep allows the Grizzlies to conserve energy.

Their heart rate slows down from 40 beats per minute to 8 — 12 beats. They also use 50% less oxygen.

Both males and females will use the same general area to make their dens year after year. The exact same den is not used more than once.

True Hibernation or something else?

Scientists are not sure whether to call a Grizzly's winter sleep true hibernation.

True hibernators, like the Ground Squirrel, drop their body temperature to almost freezing when they hibernate. Grizzlies hardly lower their body temperatures.

Grizzlies are very quick to wake up after their hibernation. True hibernators are very slow to wake up after hibernation.

True hibernators will sleep through loud noises. Grizzlies can wake up easily if disturbed.

Because of these differences, some scientists say that the sleep that Grizzlies go into every Winter should be called "denning" instead of hibernation.

How do Grizzlies communicate with one another?

Grizzly bears use growls, roars and snorts to communicate with each other.

Other sounds they make are snorting, huffing, clacking teeth, popping the jaw or blowing air out of their nostrils.

A male Grizzly rubs his back, head or chest against a tree to mark it with his scent to let other males know that he is in the area.

A Grizzly will also mark and scratch trees on the bark to alert other bears that he is around.

Are Grizzlies dangerous?

Grizzly bears normally avoid contact with people.

Even though Grizzlies are so much larger and stronger than humans, they almost never think of humans as prey and don't normally hunt them.

In more than 70% of fatal attacks on humans, a Grizzly bear mother was defending her cubs from what she thought was danger.

Many Grizzly bear attacks result when a bear has been surprised by humans at very close range.

A Grizzly will fight more ferociously and be more aggressive than any other animal when it believes it needs to protect itself or its cubs. This is where the Grizzly gets its reputation for being so dangerous.

Grizzly Fun Facts

1. A Grizzly bear has a better sense of smell than a hunting dog. When the wind is blowing towards them, Grizzlies can smell a dead animal from 20 miles (30 km) away.

2. Grizzlies are good swimmers. Grizzlies in coastal areas have been known to hunt seals by swimming in the sea. Swimming across a river or a lake is easy for these bears. During the heat of Summer Grizzlies have been seen cooling off in water just as we humans do.

3. Unlike other animals like Cats and Dogs, Grizzlies see in full color, just like humans. Grizzlies also have excellent night vision, which is better than humans.

4. Grizzlies have such a powerful bite they could crush a bowling ball in their jaws.

THANKS FOR READING!

Please leave a review at the website where you bought this book and tell others what you liked about it.

Visit www.TJRob.com for a FREE eBook and to see TJ Rob's other exciting books

  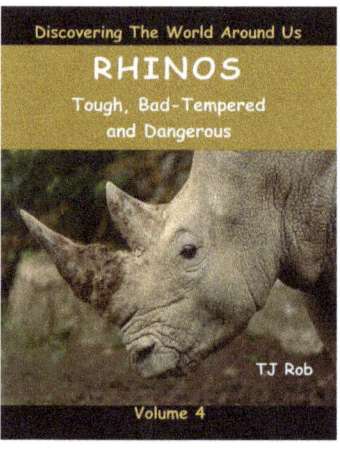 

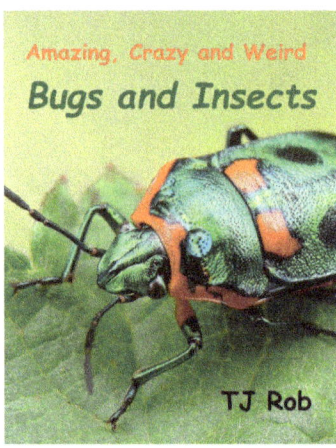  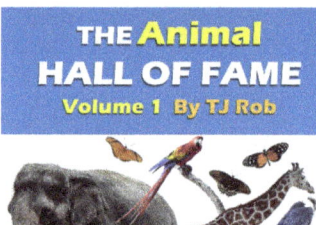   

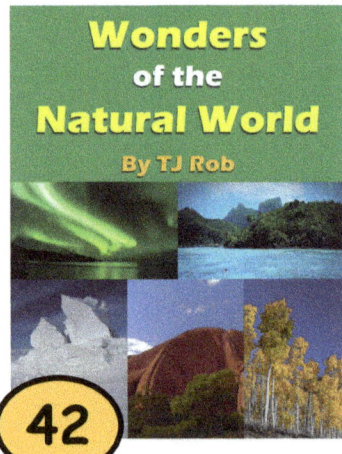 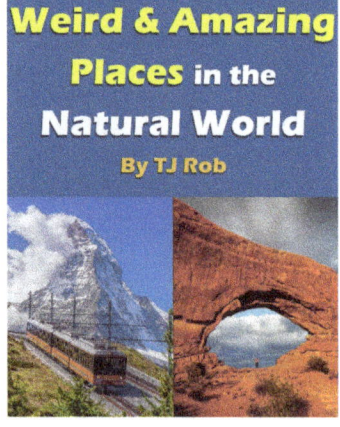  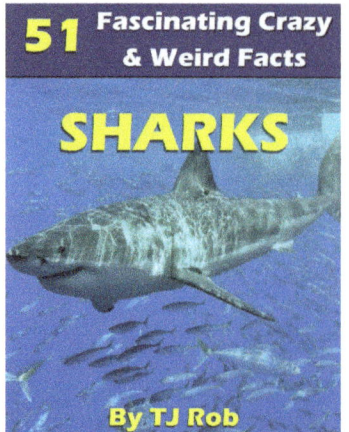

www.ingramcontent.com/pod-product-compliance
Lightning Source LLC
Chambersburg PA
CBHW040004080526
44586CB00027B/2881